Why Artists suffer in pain and Tragedy

Table of contents

b. My own suffering

c. The pain of being an artist

Artists, big or small, tend to suffer, maybe it is a curse to be creative with so many artists like me who die untimely, live in poverty and just plain addicted to drugs and bad luck...... let me give you some examples.....

1, Elvis Presley 1935-1977, the deep-fried king of rock n roll was the most successful

entertainer of
his generation
yet his
addiction to
prescription
drugs was a

curse that led to his demise. However the deep fried king will always be remembered

for his great talents and achievements

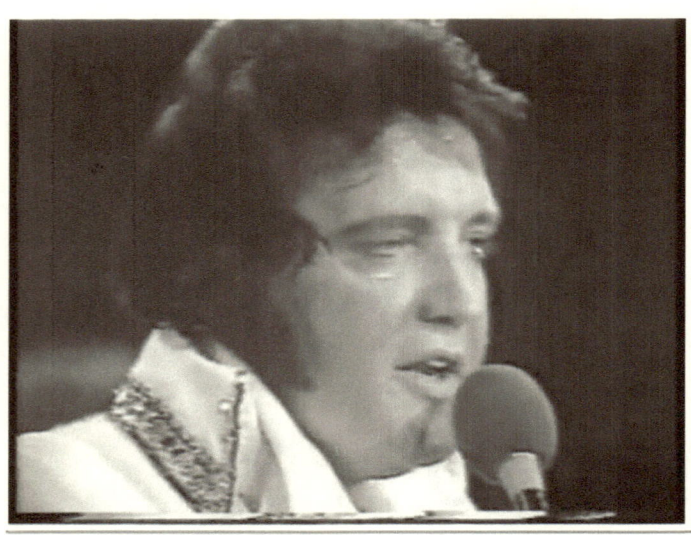

2. Jimi Hendrix

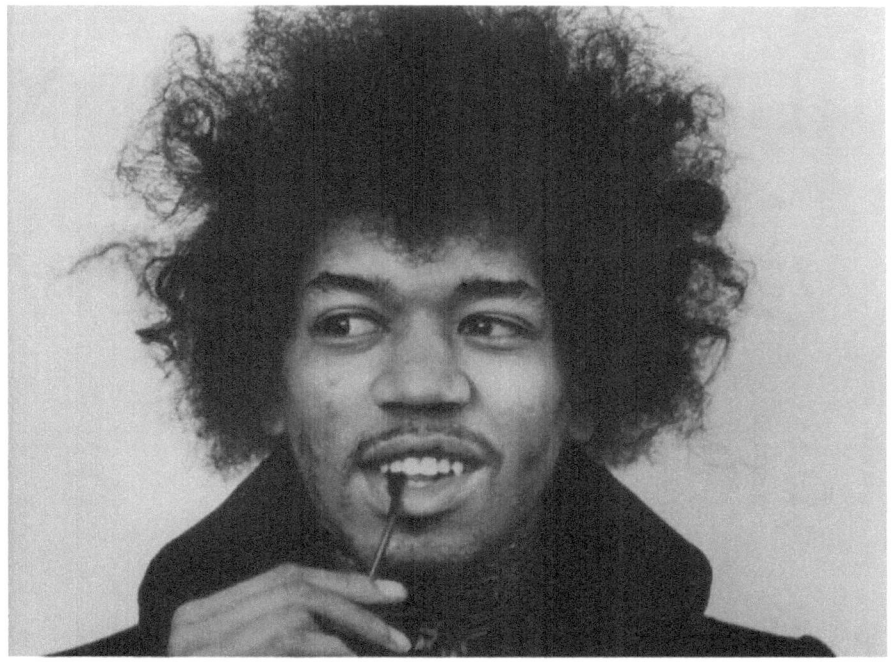

Jimi Hendrix was extremely talented at playing rock guitar to the point where he was able to expand the vocabulary of the rock guitar, paving the way for hard rock, heavy metal as well as expand the funk category which led, by his influence, to prince. Jimi however suffered for his art through drug and alcohol addictions as well as being ripped off by his manager, Michael Jeffrey.

Jimi also had to deal with other business manipulations and racism because of

what he wore
and who he
hung out with.
He will always
be one of the
greatest

guitarists in rock and metal history.

Other examples and there are

numerous, like van Gogh who cut his ear off and was harassed by others. Vincent

Van Gogh suffered from mental illness and poverty as he committed suicide in 1890.

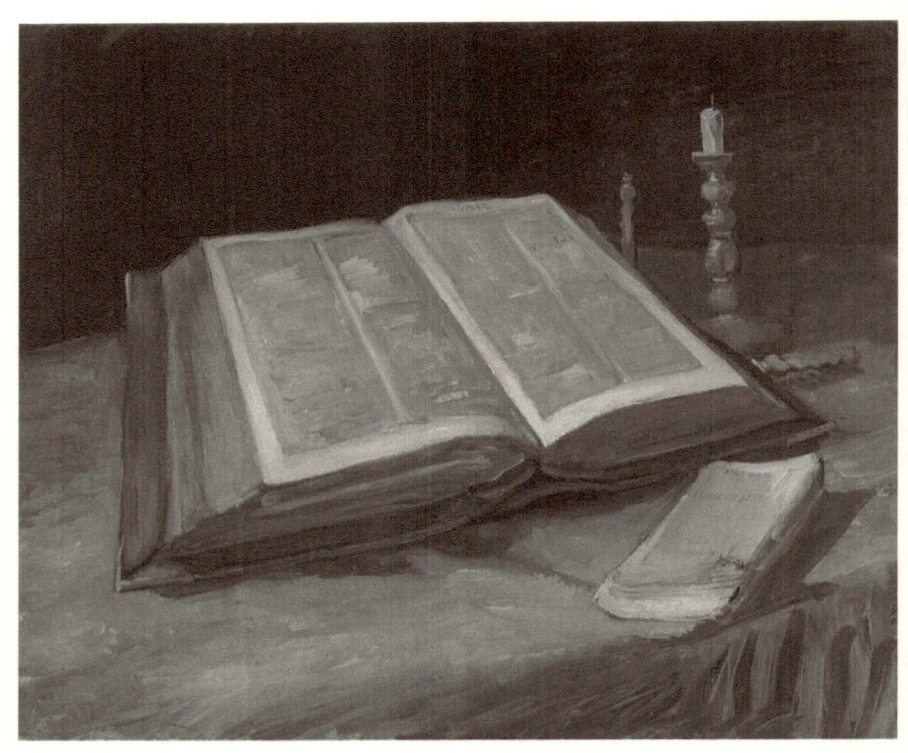

Picture above

by van Gogh

and picture below of van Gogh was diagnosed with bipolar disorder

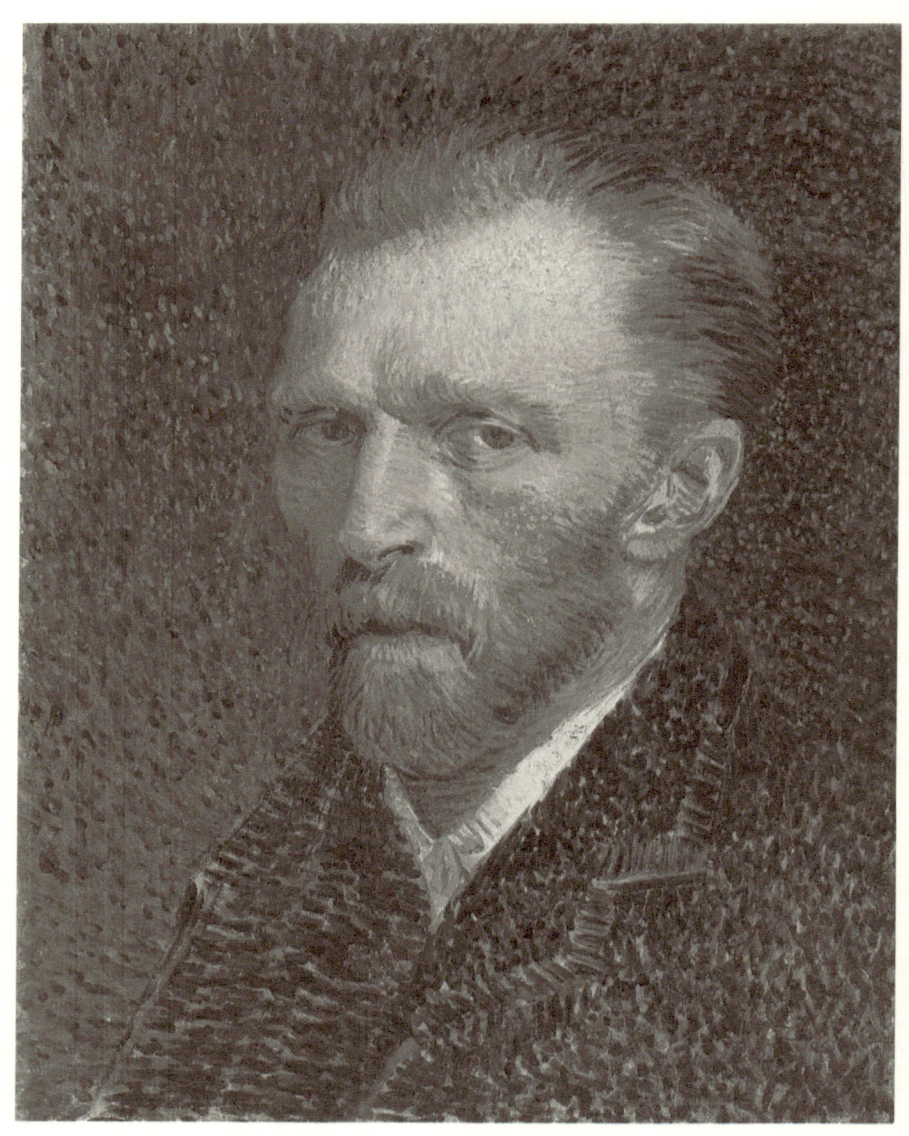

Robin Williams 1951-2014 was a great comedian, actor and Oscar winner

however Robin
suffered from
physical
illnesses and
pressures
which lead to

his suicide in 2014. Robin Williams also suffered past bouts of alcoholism and lewd body dementia Whitney Houston 1963-2012 was a phenomenal singer in pop music however pressures with her marriage to bobby brown, and alcohol and cocaine addictions led to her untimely death in 2012.

Many singers have died

untimely due to addictions, murder, mental illness and suicide.

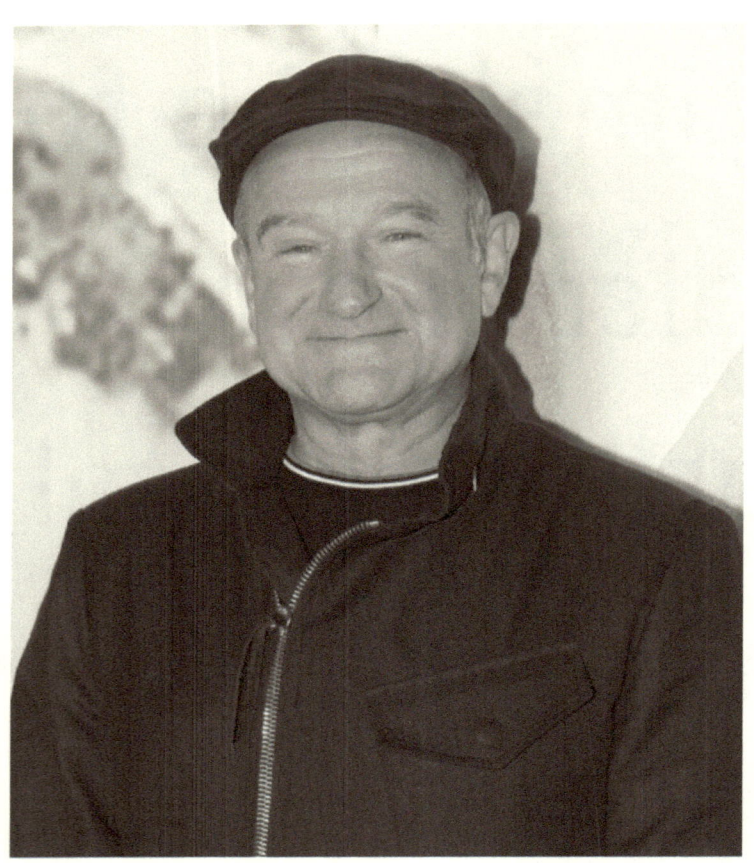

Robin Williams

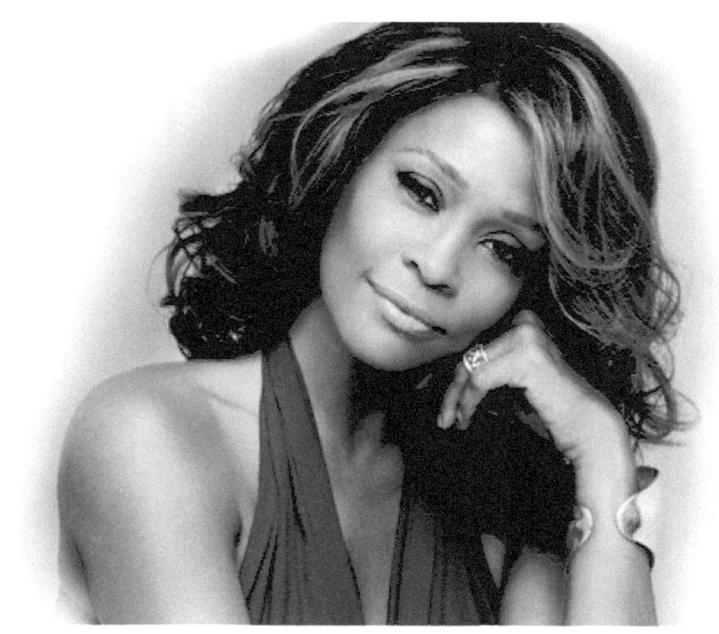

Whitney Houston

No myth of the tortured artist

Many artists, from Kurt cocaine, to river phoenix to

Jim Morrison were tortured souls who turned to their art to deal with their drug addictions, bad childhoods and mental illnesses .There are many actors, painters, musicians and novelists who suffered from many painful events which inspired them

to be artists.
The other side
of it is that
many lost their
lives tragically.
Marvin Gaye

had drug addictions and was murdered by his dad. Michael Jackson had

suffered
accusations of
child abuse,
drug addictions
which led him
to his untimely

death by drug addiction.

John Lennon was murdered by an obsessive fan but

suffered in his lifetime from the loss of his mother and drug addiction.

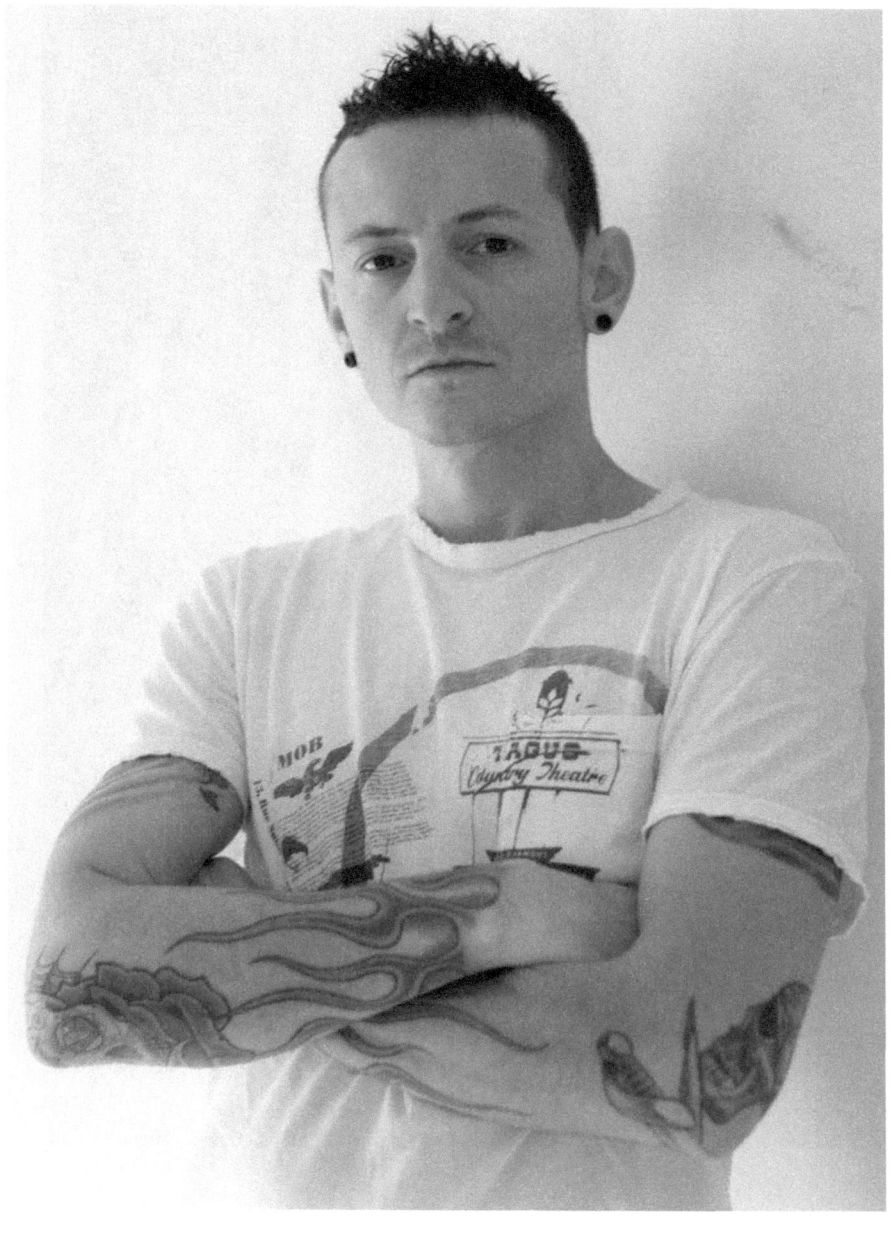

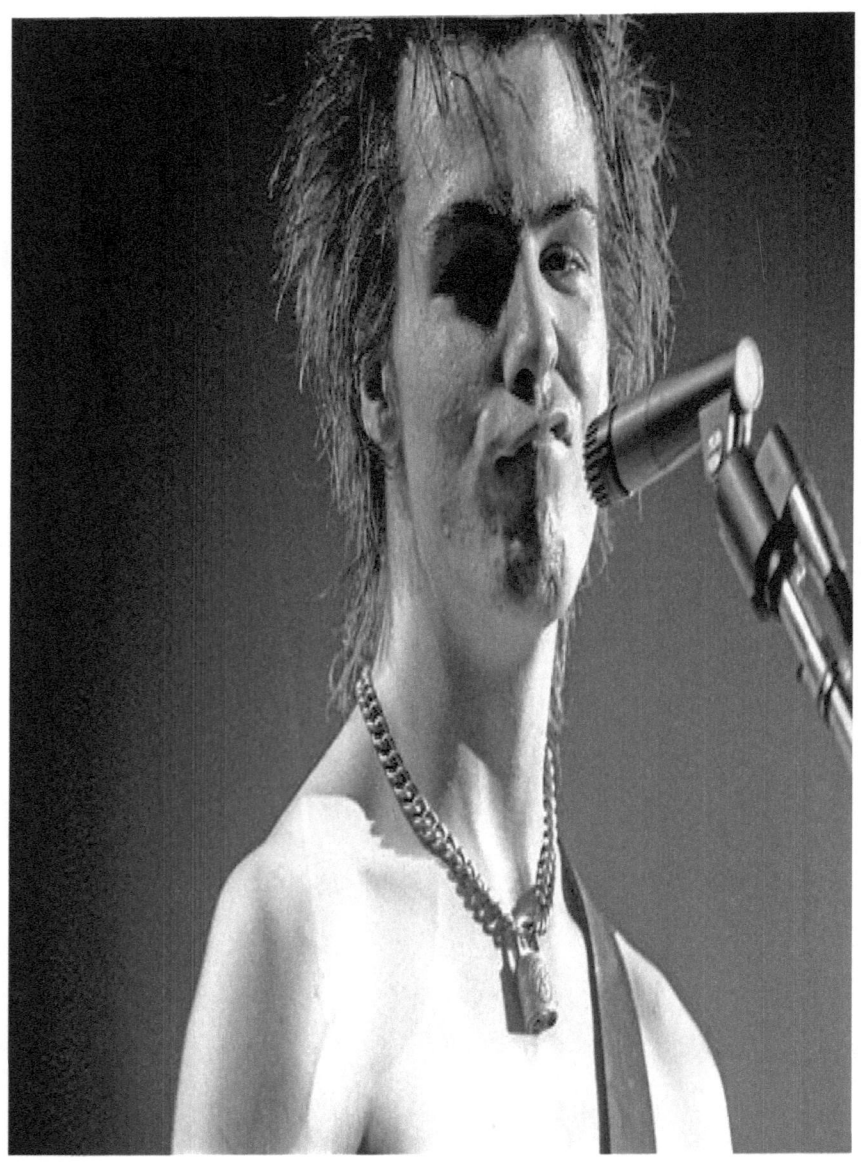

Sid vicious (above) died of a drug overdose after allegedly murdering his girlfriend and growing up with a drug-addicted mother.

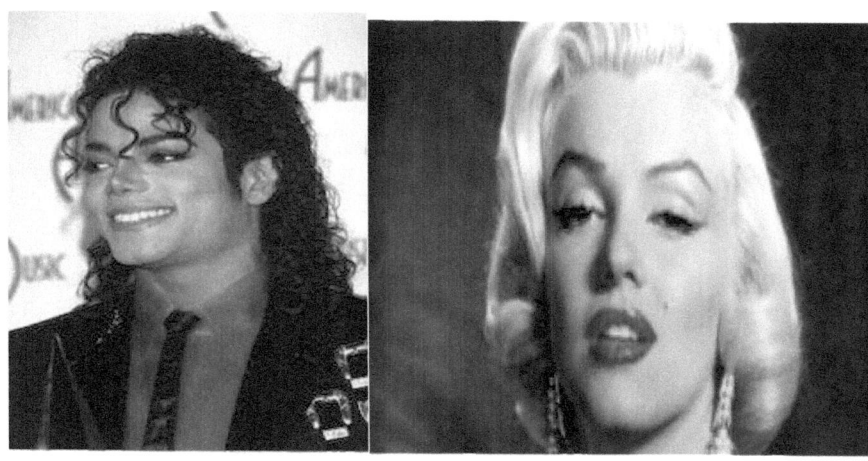

Countless

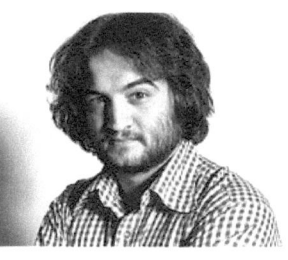

tragedies

48

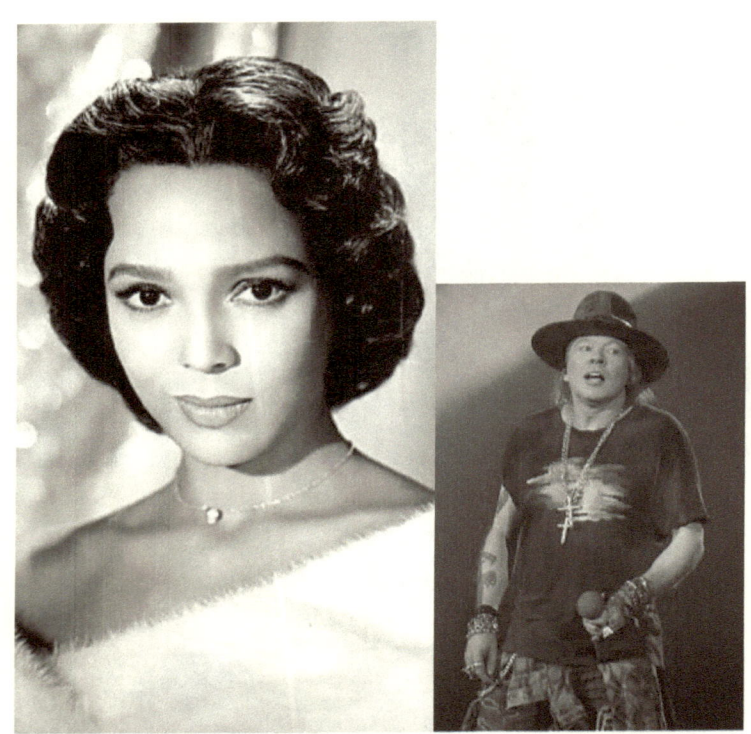

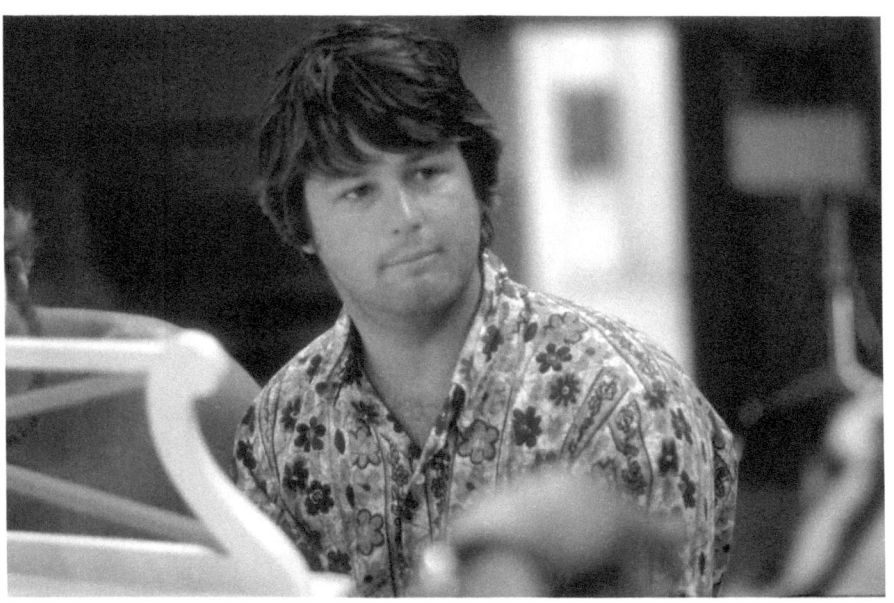

bad childhoods

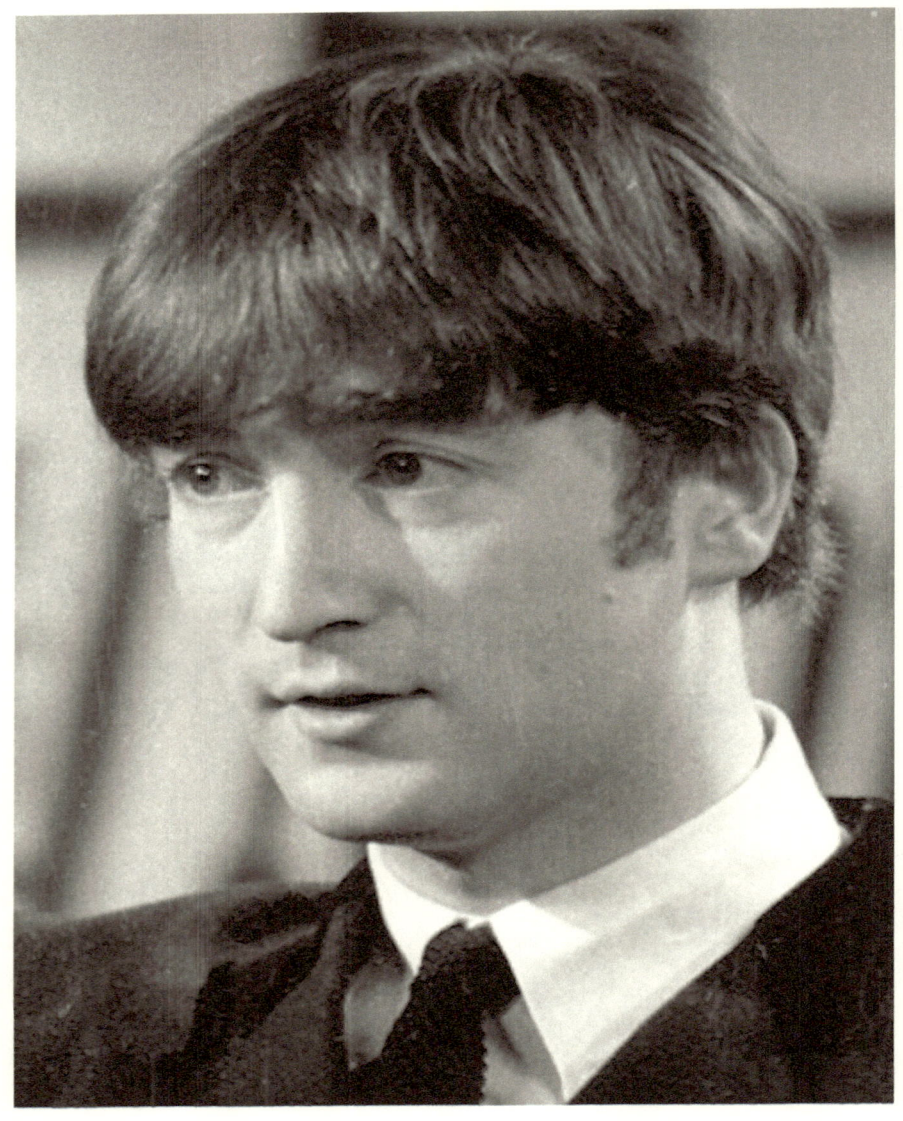

Chris farley comedian died of drug overdose   janis joplin musician died of drug overdose

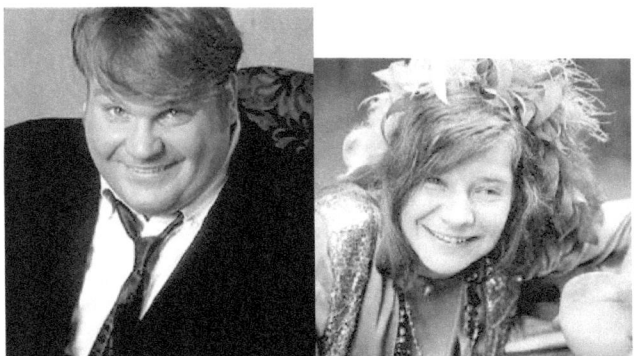

jim morrison died untimely in 1971

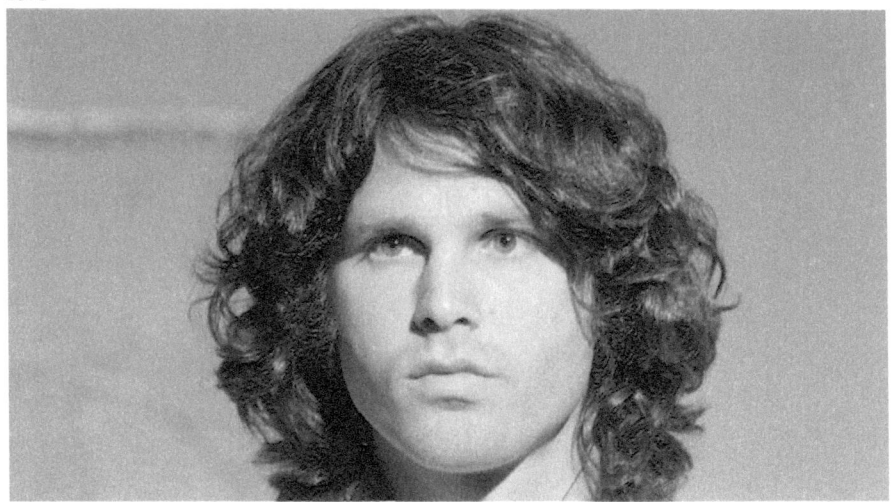

Sylvia path (poet) killed herself by putting her head into an oven suffered depression

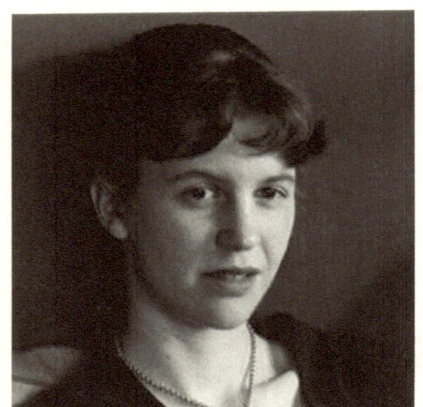

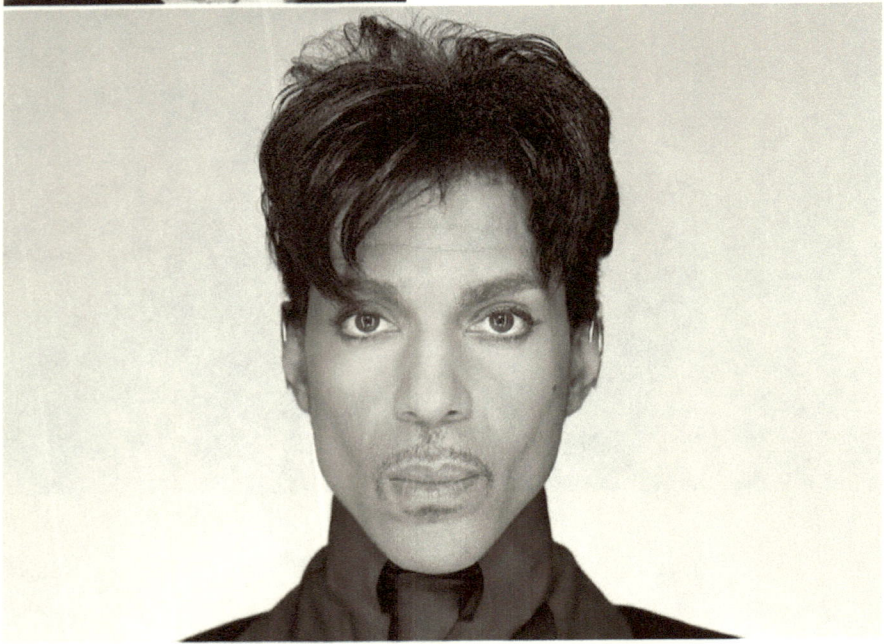

Prince (musician died of drug overdose in 2016

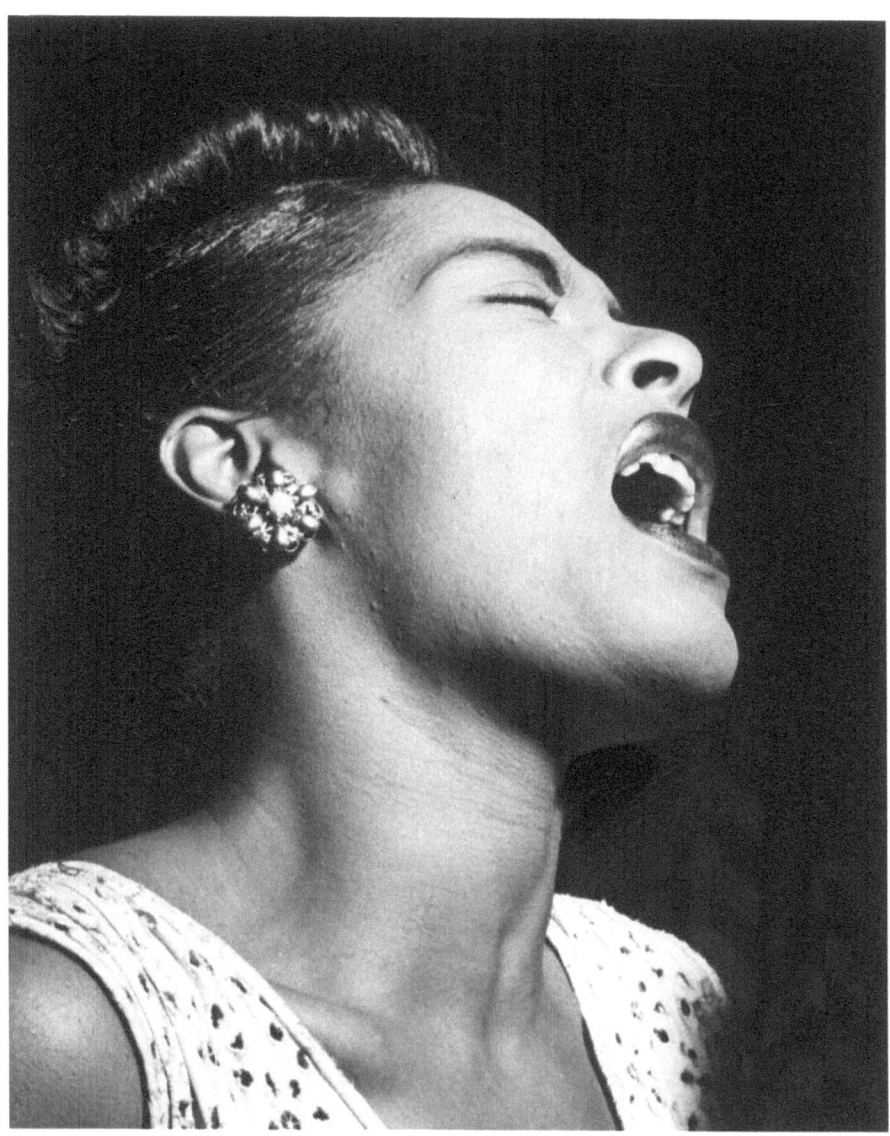

Billie holiday struggled with drug addiction leading to her untimely death in 1959

Mental health of many artists ,poets, sculptors , singers, you name it ,have been noted , Kurt cobain, guitarist ,singer from nirvana who killed himself ,suffered from bipolar disorder

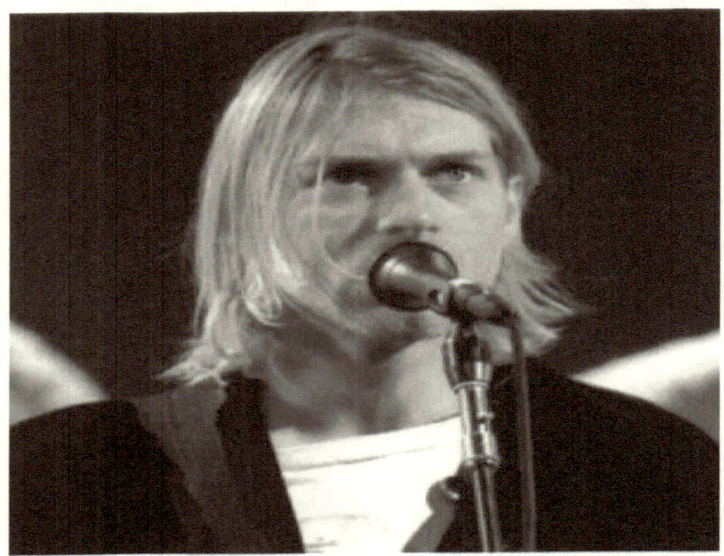

Marilyn Monroe suffered from mental illness and drug addiction when she died in 1962

Tragedies

Broken

relationships

Drug addictions

Mental

illnesses

Untimely deaths

B.My own suffering

I had a very bad childhood

where abuse
was rampant
towards me, I
turn to drawing
pictures when
young, and I

then turn to singing due to being an outcast, harassment as a teenager. I

never had love
or felt it so I
wrote about it
in my songs,
like trauma yet
I aspire to

break the curse of being an artist troubled by events out of my control. I live in poverty,

being harassed
because of
jealousy
jealous people
trying or have
stolen my

songs like I want to be with you, trying to stop me from succeeding, feeling ignored, rejected, and cursed with bad experiences, harassment, no true love relationships

and deprived of
a real life
despite being
An inspired
artist.

C.pain of being an artist, I for one can relate because I had some bad experiences

that I use to
write in lyrics in
my songs. Pain
has inspired a
lot of artists.
However for

me, I now would like to write songs, or create through more positive expressions. I now believe

being positive

and healthy is

the key, despite

the lack thereof

in my life, keep

hope alive,
positivity in my
life and reality
about it is the
way.

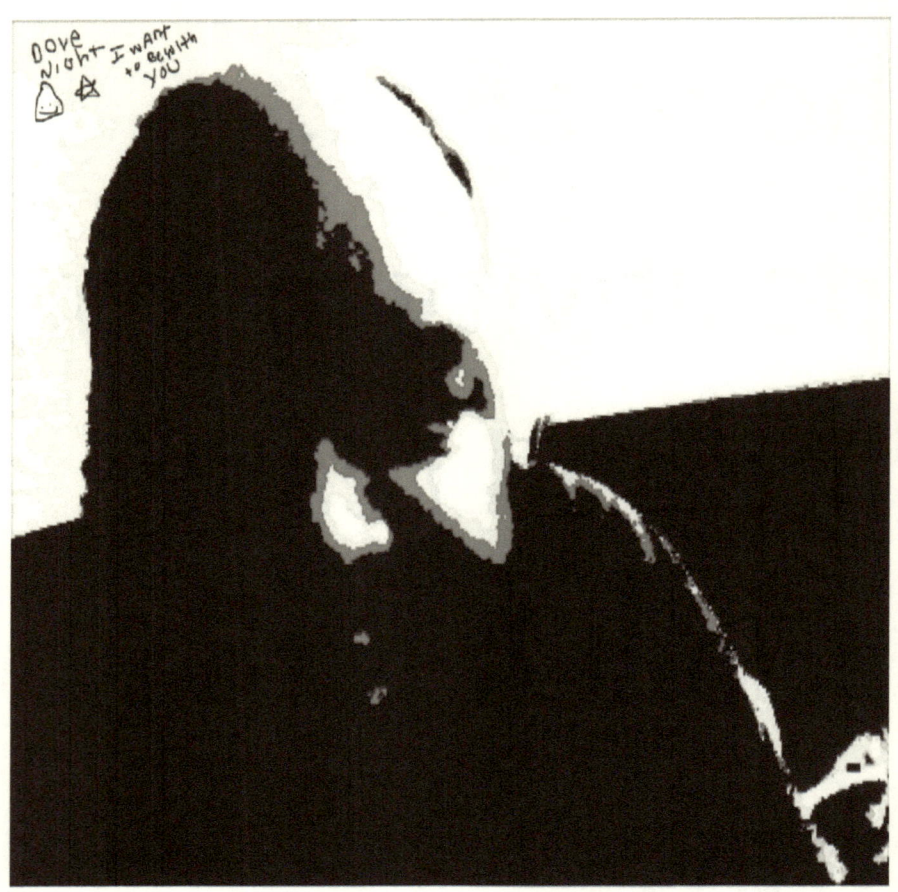

Dove night

www.ingramcontent.com/pod-product-compliance
Lightning Source LLC
Chambersburg PA
CBHW021903170526
45157CB00005B/1950